THE OTHER SIDE OF CAMPUS LIFE

THE OTHER SIDE OF CAMPUS LIFE

A Parent and Student Guide to Campus Safety
told through the eyes of former campus Chief of Police

DAVID HELTON

DIRECTOR, POLICE AND PUBLIC SAFETY (RETIRED)

authorHOUSE®

AuthorHouse™ LLC
1663 Liberty Drive
Bloomington, IN 47403
www.authorhouse.com
Phone: 1-800-839-8640

Published by AuthorHouse   02/05/2014

ISBN: 978-1-4918-5295-8 (sc)
ISBN: 978-1-4918-5294-1 (hc)
ISBN: 978-1-4918-5293-4 (e)

Library of Congress Control Number: 2014901719

For Kristin and Jerica—I could not be more proud of you both

~ and ~

For all those students, faculty, and staff who made
my law enforcement career so rewarding

CONTENTS

FOREWORD

Oftentimes, colleges and universities fail to prepare prospective students for all that accompanies everyday life in a college setting. It is my hope that the material contained herein will illuminate some of these issues to improve the overall college experience.

For almost thirty years, I had the opportunity to serve at two separate college law-enforcement agencies: sixteen years at a private, 4-year liberal arts college and thirteen years at a 4-year, state-funded university. For the latter two decades, I served as chief of campus police, before retiring at the age of fifty-five.

I carefully considered how to present my experiences in both an educational and entertaining manner, before I made the decision to abandon the path of previous campus crime authors. Namely, I do not use statistics to validate my points. My rationale for this is that incoming freshmen do not need to burden themselves with crime statistics. Statistics, while useful for many purposes, do not provide a complete picture on their own. Therefore, I have chosen to present real-life situations I encountered throughout my college law-enforcement career.

I hope you both enjoy, and learn from, the information that follows. All of the anecdotes described in this book are real; all of the student names are fictitious.

Yours truly,

David Helton, Director Police and Public Safety (Retired)

INTRODUCTION

A good prank is well and good—that is, until someone finds out about it. As a younger man, that someone was usually my mother, who would promptly report the incident to my father when he arrived home from work. I remember listening quietly while he lectured me, shaking his head as he washed his hands at the kitchen sink before dinner. He never raised his voice or made threats; he simply stated his case and wrapped it up with the well-known adage that, "it is okay to make a mistake as long as you learn a lesson from it". Then my father would dry his hands on an old dishtowel and add, "but it's better to let someone *else* make the mistake—then, learn from *that*."

It took a long time before I truly understood what he meant by that; however, it is in the same spirit I offer the information in this book. Take the mistakes made by these students and learn not only valuable lessons, but also how to protect yourself as a student.

Life on a college campus is often far more complex than taking a chemistry exam, researching a term paper, or preparing for finals. If you enter college with the mindset that you only need to go to class and pass some tests, then you are going to fail. Campus life is a total learning experience. Those who successfully complete the process are fortunate to do so without encountering a negative life experience along the way.

During my tenure as a campus police officer, I learned to expect the unexpected. While most of the negative situations you will read about involved a relatively small percentage of the campus population, what this small percentage of students could do on any given day would amaze you.

They surprised me every day for thirty years.

THE CLERY ACT[1]

You will want to remember this.

On April 5, 1986, Lehigh University freshman, Jeanne Ann Clery, was raped and murdered as she slept in her dorm room. She was nineteen years old.

Following their daughter's murder, Howard and Connie Clery discovered that Lehigh University administrators failed to inform students of a significant number of violent crimes occurring in the three years prior to Jeanne's attack. In hopes to prevent another tragedy, the Clery's joined forces with other victims of campus crime to persuade Congress to take measures to better inform and protect students. Their efforts resulted in what was originally known as the *Crime Awareness and Campus Security Act of 1990*. Later, this law would become known as the *Jeanne Clery Disclosure of Campus Security Policy and Campus Crime Statistics Act (20 USC § 1092(f))*.

The *Jeanne Clery Disclosure of Campus Security Policy and Campus Crime Statistics Act* revolutionized the way campus law enforcement agencies nationwide handled (and reported) campus crime. Rather quickly, archaic security operations prevalent in the 1970's and 1980's were replaced with modern, professional law enforcement agencies. Prior to the Clery Act, colleges and universities could choose which crimes to report, if they chose to report them at all. After the passage of the Clery Act, federal law dictated that campus crime be reported to students and parents.

This, in my opinion, is the single most important aspect of the law. Before the Clery Act, I observed senior administrators clearly indicating that an incident was not to be reported to the public, nor pursued through the criminal justice system.

---

[1]   2012 Clery Center for Security On Campus, Inc. (2012). *Summary of the jeanne clery act*. Retrieved from http://clerycenter.org/

However, after the Act passed, a few administrators chose to use the legislation in a positive manner, by offering the public full-disclosure of all incidents that occurred on campus. The Clery Act, along with support from administration, became a great tool in bolstering crime prevention efforts on campuses across the nation. Despite the passage of the Clery Act, however, I observed administrators who still chose to bury information when they thought it was in the best interest of the university. Thankfully, these times were rare, and I was typically able to lead my campus police departments in a manner that complied with federal regulations.

The process of requiring full-disclosure regarding campus crime did not come easily, or without a price. At the time I was first appointed to lead a campus law enforcement agency, a nationally read publication distributed a questionnaire to campus police departments, asking them to report campus crime statistics. Although I felt compelled to complete the questionnaire, I did not. I was not so much concerned about reporting the crime statistics for our campus; rather, I was concerned that other colleges and universities would not report their statistics honestly.

Unfortunately, my concerns were legitimate. A chief of police for a major university completed the questionnaire in an honest and accurate manner, and shortly afterwards, was informed that his campus was rated the most dangerous in the country. It was not, by any stretch of the imagination, but he was one of those who reported honestly and accurately. News of his retirement came shortly after the article went to press.

The Clery Act requires colleges and universities to publish crime statistics each year, but do not assume that the statistics you see are one-hundred percent accurate. Even when threatened with federal legislation, some schools choose not to report everything that occurs. The Clery family founded a non-profit organization known as Security on Campus (SOC). I would encourage parents and students to visit the organization's website at http://www.securityoncampus.org/ to read about campus crime in detail. Not only does this organization offer tremendous insight into campus life, parents and students can call upon the organization to help if problems do occur on campus. SOC oftentimes will begin investigations into crimes that occur on college campuses and then provide their findings to the United States Department of Education. When this federal agency begins checking into concerns raised by SOC, colleges and universities take note, as federal funding could be at risk.

Another great way for parents and students to acquire a true sense of the campus atmosphere is to schedule an impromptu visit to the school, rather than basing an impression on a single weekend orientation when everyone is on his or her best behavior. Check out the school newspaper archives to see what has happened in the past year on and around campus, what the relationships are like between the campus police and student affairs, and about information reported on the cafeteria.

If the campus police department is not mentioned in any articles in the past year, be alarmed. There should be positive reports of their crime prevention efforts, as well as information on newly developed programs designed to keep the campus safe. There should even be articles wherein the paper disagrees with a response the campus police gave to a situation. This shows that both entities, the paper and the police, are doing their respective jobs to the best of their ability. The bottom line is that one should beware of any campus with no reported issues. It is okay to have problems. The important thing is that corrective action is taken to prevent future concerns.

PART ONE

GETTING SETTLED ON CAMPUS

CHAPTER 1

ORIENTATION

ost colleges and universities schedule a two-day summer orientation session to provide parents and incoming freshmen an opportunity to learn more about the campus. The goal is to familiarize prospective students with campus life and to make a smooth transition from living at home to living on-campus. What parents and students should realize when they attend these summer orientations is the schools are still in selling mode; they are putting their best foot forward in order to seal the deal. They want to guarantee that you and your child have an enjoyable experience and, in turn, enroll for classes in the fall semester. It might be an institution of higher learning, but in the end, it is simply a business with a product to sell.

I always enjoyed meeting and speaking with parents and students during summer orientation sessions, as it provided me an opportunity to outline the dangers of campus living and discuss some of the situations students have encountered in the past. I firmly believe that this time spent with parents and students was an essential part of any orientation session. It equipped parents and students with necessary information to ensure they stayed safe in the campus community. The time allotted for these meetings varied between the two schools I served. I do not think it had anything to do with one being a private college and the other one being state-funded; instead, it had everything to do with the personalities of the administration that managed new-student orientations.

The private college I worked for had an administration that believed providing a safe campus environment involved educating parents and students about issues and problems that might occur. The state-funded university, on the other hand, had an administration that believed telling parents and students too much was bad for business. Naturally, at the private college, I always had one to two hours allotted to speak with parents and students, while the state-funded university allotted ten to fifteen minutes.

At the private college, there was no censorship on the information I shared; the administration trusted my good judgment to provide useful information without sounding pessimistic in the process. This college was exceptionally proactive when it came to developing and maintaining a safe campus environment. The state-funded university had a different set of ideals.

One conversation in particular comes to mind. I had just concluded a session on campus safety, when a senior administrator stopped me and warned against sharing too much information. I remember him saying, "These parents haven't decided to send their kids here yet, and we can't have you frightening them away."

I replied, "But what about keeping them safe once they get here? I have a responsibility to these people."

To that, he answered, "No, you have a responsibility to this school."

I never believed the presentations I provided at the state-funded university were anything more than well-rehearsed puppet shows. I believed I was doing a disservice to parents and their children by not speaking with them in more detail. In order to offset this unfortunate censorship, I would usually arrive well before the presentation, and make myself available afterward, in hopes that parents or students would approach me and ask questions.

I will offer this advice. Whenever you attend a new-student orientation, there are key questions you should ask during open sessions. A college or university should be forthcoming with any information that would help you in the decision to allow your child to attend. The responses, or lack thereof, will also tell you how important the college or university considers campus safety.

What Questions Should I Ask?

You may not know what questions to ask during campus safety sessions, and that is okay. Here are questions you may wish to use:

- Campus Code Violations—Does the campus publish a list of campus judiciary charges and the outcome of each? Is this information available to the public on the school website? By federal law (see, *The Clery Act*) the college and university should disclose this information.
- Arrests—Does the campus police department publish crime statistics in compliance with federal law (see, *The Clery Act*) and is this available to the public on a website?
- Drugs and Alcohol—Does the campus have a problem with drugs and/or alcohol? If anyone ever tells you their campus does not have problems, there is no need to listen to another word they say. Every college and university, just like the community in which you live, has some degree of drug and alcohol issues. It is not so important whether they have a problem, but whether or not the school recognizes the problem and takes proactive measures to prevent future issues.
- Escort Services—Does the campus have a mechanism in place to escort students to and from campus facilities after normal business hours? Is the schedule posted for students?
- Visitation—Is there 24-hour visitation in the residence halls? What means of control is present to ensure the safety of both female and male students? Do the residence halls have limited access points? Are residence-life staff members assigned to work in the halls? Do the halls have closed-captioned televisions (CCTV's) in various public locations in and around the dorms?
- Town—Gown Relationships—For those who may not know, the term *town-gown* relates to the relations between a town and the university located within the town; the relations between

university students and the nonstudents who live in a university town[2].

Now that you know what it means, you can ask questions relative to town-gown relationships. Questions such as:

o Have there been any issues in the past between students and neighboring non-students?
o What is the relationship between the local police department and the campus police department?
o Are crime statistics available for the surrounding town in which the college or university is located?

The Clery Act requires colleges and universities to publish these statistics, as well as those that happen on campus. Many times, students are victims to crime that occurs in the local community. Read the archives from local newspapers and campus newspapers to become aware of dangers lurking outside the confines of the campus community. Speak with upperclassmen when visiting the campus to see what their thoughts are of the local community.

• Parking on Campus—Are there sufficient numbers of safe, close convenient parking spaces for students? Most colleges and universities do not have close, convenient spaces for everyone. In my opinion, female resident students should have the closest, safest, most convenient parking spaces, but then so should commuters who take night classes. Students should not be expected to walk too far late at night, especially if the campus is not well lit. How many tickets are issued annually to students? Is there an appeal system in place for students? Are faculty and staff required to purchase parking permits and pay parking fines? Students typically pay the largest percentage of the total costs for parking enforcement operations, but faculty and staff should be responsible too.

---

2   town-and-gown. (n.d.) *McGraw-Hill Dictionary of American Idioms and Phrasal Verbs.* (2002). Retrieved October 4 2013 from http://idioms. thefreedictionary.com/town-and-gown

- <u>24-Hour Police Protection</u>—Is the campus protected by a full-time law enforcement agency that provides around the clock protection and immediate response to calls for assistance? Do the students have a means to contact police twenty-four hours a day and actually speak with someone on the phone? If a student visits the police department, will the doors always be open and will someone physically be there to provide assistance? How many police are on duty each shift?

The reason for asking questions such as these is simple. At the private college, our police force was limited such that we only had one police officer working most shifts, with the exception of over-lapping coverage on weeknights from 10pm-2am. The force was supplemented with student security officers. Local police were available to assist if a situation deemed it necessary, but their loyalties were to the municipality in which they were employed, not the college. This created conflict at times.

At the state-funded university, more funding was available. At least three to four police officers worked each shift, with up to seven officers working Thursday nights, which is typically the party night on college and university campuses.

- <u>Early Warning</u>—Is there a system in place so that police can notify the campus community of dangerous situations as they are occurring? Does the college provide a demonstration? There are various notification systems available that campus police can use to contact students via phone, email, and/or text messaging. Ask if the campus you are visiting has these capabilities. Do campus police post bulletins in high profile areas around the campus to alert students of recent criminal activity? For instance, if an armed robbery occurs on a street nearby the campus, are students notified and forewarned to use extreme caution.
- <u>CCTV's</u>—Are there cameras in place at residence halls, classroom buildings, and various areas throughout the campus such as automated teller machines (ATM's), the bookstore, or remote walking paths? Cameras do not prevent all crime from occurring, but they contribute to the overall campus safety.

Campus police are able to solve a number of crimes each school year as a direct result of images captured on cameras.

- <u>Crisis Prevention/Disaster Response</u>—Is there a system in place to prevent and/or respond to crises that occur on campus? Are there routine drills conducted to educate the campus in appropriate responses to emergencies? Are students well informed of the <u>safe</u> areas on campus if an emergency occurs? Is there a 24-hour number for parents and other family members to call during a crisis to find out about the safety of their child?

- <u>Code Blue Telephones</u>—Are code-blue telephones available throughout the campus for student emergencies? Are they located in conspicuous areas and tested regularly to ensure they are functioning correctly? During some of our regular tests, we found problems with the emergency phones. A campus should not assume the phones work; regular testing provides a reasonable assurance that the phone is operational should an emergency arise.

- <u>Lighting</u>—Is the campus well lit at night? Whether you realize it or not, security lighting plays a key role in protecting students. Take a walk around the campus in the evening hours. If you cannot see clearly, it is too dark. Campuses that place emphasis on safety usually maintain a well-lit campus, especially around residence halls and classroom buildings.

Most importantly, if you are planning to attend an orientation session prior to enrolling, write down your questions ahead of time to ensure you will get the answers you are looking for. You may want to ask to speak with the chief of campus police while there, not only to build a relationship that might come in handy later, but also to get a feel for how this person interacts with others and what his/her philosophy is concerning campus safety.

CHAPTER 2

CAMPUS ORGANIZATIONS AND ESTABLISHING RELATIONSHIPS

W hen parents send their children off to college, they often caution them not to become involved in extra-curricular activities at first. The emphasis is on studies rather than socialization. Study, study, and then study some more is the creed. Largely, I agree with this philosophy. Many students cannot handle the responsibilities that come with balancing classroom and extra-curricular activities.

Whenever I had the opportunity to speak with parents during orientation sessions, I always encouraged them to allow their student to become involved in campus organizations and activities. I could tell that some parents were reluctant to accept my thought process, as people naturally assume that athletics are the only activities available on a college campus. This is far from the truth. There are actually very few opportunities to participate in college athletics compared to the abundant number of other rewarding activities available. There are fraternities and sororities, civic organizations, internships, professor assistantships, and work-study opportunities.

I am sure many of you have heard horror stories about fraternities and sororities on campuses across the country, and to be honest, some of them are true. An instance comes to mind whenever a parent asks about their student becoming involved in such organizations. This one, in particular, involved drinking and bullying to the extent that administration forbade the fraternity to function on campus. This is an exception and not the norm.

Many fraternities and sororities have a positive influence on the campus and surrounding community. If your child considers becoming a member of a campus organization, ask about the organization's deeds. An organization that is proactive in efforts to have a positive effect within campus and the community is one worth considering.

There are other alternatives to clubs or civic organizations. Many students choose to participate in work-study assignments. As chief of police, I employed more than one-hundred students as part of the work-study initiatives. Some of these students came through the financial aid department and worked throughout the four years of their college careers, while others served as interns. Many of these students pursued criminal justice careers upon graduating.

There was never a student, under my leadership, harmed or injured in any way. I made a conscious effort to limit student involvement in situations where one could expect to encounter physical harm. Most student workers performed tasks related to building security or dispatching. Some students eventually became more involved in crime prevention roles, but even then, they were limited in their involvement with incidents where they might be harmed.

You have to realize too, that if, by chance, a student does make an error in judgment along the way and finds himself/herself in some sort of trouble it, surely makes good sense to have a support team close at hand. I have seen many students who encountered a problem and had the good fortune of having a professor or department staff member step in to offer assistance, guidance, or perhaps even a voice that swayed the outcome in a positive manner.

In this light, can you imagine the benefits of having a son or daughter working with the campus police? Encourage your child to build relationships within other areas of the campus, as well. Some examples include:

- Vice-Chancellor/Vice President within the Business and Finance Division (which can prove helpful when faced with hefty fines or unpaid fees): I cannot tell you the times when a parent or student would go over my head and convince one of these key administrators to void or reduce a parking fine, waive a fee, or allow additional time in which to pay.

- <u>Vice Chancellor/Vice-President within Student Affairs</u>: There were more than a few times when I observed a concerned parent visit campus and suddenly a student who appeared on the brink of being expelled received a more favorable outcome.

You may think that having your child develop relationships with seemingly unimportant role players on a campus is not very important, but I would suggest the time invested is worth it. I would suggest that you find out who the following people are in these positions.

- <u>Chancellor/President's Administrative Assistant:</u> This is a person who has direct contact with the boss every day. Those of us who have worked on a campus know how important it is to become acquainted with this administrative assistant in a positive way. At the private college where I served under two presidents, I learned that the administrative assistant was an extremely powerful role. Those who failed to learn this lesson encountered difficulties.

Bottom line, once again, is that you are paying a great deal of money toward a college education for your son or daughter. Having your child develop a relationship with some of these key players I have mentioned is great insurance on your investment. Is it wrong to hope for influence if a situation should arise wherein your son or daughter faces significant hurdles or possibilities of being sent home? I do not think a parent should always be there to bail out a student, but they should be able to exhaust their options if the opportunity presents itself.

CHAPTER 3

CAMPUS HOUSING

Many schools require freshmen to live on campus, at least for the first semester. Part of reason is to help students participate in the overall college experience. What the schools may not tell you is that having a resident student also generates money, as they are also required to participate in a cafeteria meal plan.

In my opinion, the campus residence experience is something in which every traditional freshman student, those coming directly from high school, should be required to participate in. I have seen issues result when older freshmen are housed with the traditional students, primarily with alcohol. It is a good thing that most freshmen are not of the legal age to consume alcohol. This makes it easier for college officials and campus police to monitor the happenings within freshmen dorms and on the campus. Living on campus is typically far less expensive than renting off-campus and, I would offer, it is generally safer, as well. Most campuses have 24-hour police protection and officers are far more readily available on campus than within the surrounding communities.

When your child moves into campus housing, and he/she is unfortunate enough to have been assigned the roommate from hell (pardon the language), there are options for remedying this. In the first two weeks of class, most dorm rooms will be booked; by the end of the second week, enough students have dropped out so that rooms are often vacant or have lost one resident. A request to the student affairs office can be all that is needed to resolve the problem, either by correcting the behavior problem that might be disturbing, or relocating one or both students. If a student makes the request and it is not immediately resolved, the parent might wish to call someone in the student affairs office, or even someone higher up on the ladder, to have the situation resolved. Roommate situations are not something that a person should take lightly, or hope that resolves itself soon. It usually does not work that way, and more problems can result.

Life off campus may be the best option for some students. Make sure that before this is agreed upon, your child is mature enough for the responsibility. Also, verify that the area in which they are hoping to move has been checked out in detail. Perhaps a call to the campus police or local police might give you an idea of what to expect in the area. The campus is required to provide you with local crime stats, which will help let you know if safety might be an issue at the particular place you are looking into.

That is what it all comes down to, safety. Will the student be safe? The answer is most definitely, yes, the vast majority of the time. Just pray that you or your child is not one those listed within crime statistics. I think it is safe to say, more times than not, students are safer on campus than in the surrounding community, or even from the communities from which they came. Residence halls, dormitories, dorms, by whatever name you wish to call the place your child will call home for four to five years, deciding upon where the student will live is a highly debated issue between parents, their child, and sometimes college/university officials.

After the first semester, or year, whichever feels right with the parents and their child (who by this time has surely become an adult), some students choose to move to an off-campus apartment. I would not recommend doing this unless the student has proven beyond any doubt that he/she can be responsible enough to flourish in that sort of environment. Unfortunately, many students want to move off campus in order to avoid campus rules and regulations regarding visitation, drugs, and alcohol. If this is the case, many times these students find in the end that living off campus is more dangerous and less conducive to obtaining an education as compared to living on campus.

In addition as to whether or not the student has proven to be responsible, safety is another key factor when considering whether to move off campus or not. Many times, students are far safer on campus. Colleges and universities, for the most part, put great effort and resources into providing a safe, secure campus. Often times, it is impossible for a local municipality to provide the same focus on safety in neighborhoods. Geography is a factor, as well as, resources in general. An example I will give is that with one school, our campus was less than two-hundred acres in size; we had three to four or more police on duty twenty-four hours a day, seven days a week. The local municipality was approximately three miles in diameter and often had only one officer on duty.

Living on campus also provides the student with a greater sense of belonging to the school, which helps in keeping them motivated to remain until graduation. Naturally, these same students are those who return to Homecomings year after year too, as they had more of a connection while enrolled.

CHAPTER 4

CAFETERIA FOOD

m ost campuses, or at least the ones I have been associated with over the years, have gone to great efforts to make the cafeteria experience a good one for students. Despite these efforts, you may hear otherwise from your child as the school year progresses. Listen to what they tell you, especially when it might pertain to cleanliness of the dining room or serving lines. Be conscious of certain factors when they might tell you that the food is terrible.

As a student, pay attention to details. Is the cafeteria kept clean at all times? Are other students consistently eating the food, or are they choosing off-campus establishments instead? Much like restaurants, the traffic in and out of the cafeteria, or lack thereof, is indicative of many things.

I always made it a point to eat in the cafeteria several times each week. As often as I could, I would visit during each of the different meal times for breakfast, lunch, and dinner. Occasionally I would visit on the weekend, just so I could witness firsthand what the students were offered during mealtime. I found, on most occasions, that the cafeteria's management did make the effort to vary the menu so students would have variety. Consider how daunting a task it is to prepare three meals a day for hundreds and hundreds of students.

As the cafeteria staff shuffles the menu to prevent students from becoming bored with the selections, you should also encourage your student to vary his/her own menu. Students should not simply walk through the buffet line at each meal, always opting for the main entrees. They should use their imagination and come up with different food combinations, from time to time. Perhaps for lunch every now and then, a salad will suffice.

Maybe a vegan diet occasionally; or, breakfast might occasionally be fruit choices, rather than the standard eggs, bacon, and sausage. If variety is the spice of life, so it is with dining in the same place for every meal.

Many schools offer different meal plans that might include limited dining at other campus food vendors. I have seen a number of fast food type restaurants on campuses. These establishments are popular for students who wish to break the monotony of dining at the same place day in and day out. If the campus does not offer such a meal plan, think about sending your child money or gift cards from time to time. A care package from home can serve the same purpose, and is usually a big hit in the residence halls where students share with friends.

CHAPTER 5

LATE NIGHT CALLS

T he students today live in a far different world than those of us who attended college back in the eighties, nineties or even ten years ago. It used to be common for students to make a date for an early dinner, a movie perhaps, and then end the evening by midnight at the latest. For the vast majority of today's student population, those curfews no longer exist.

Today, students often have an early dinner at the cafeteria with friends, return to their dorms to take care of homework, catch a nap if possible, and await phone calls from home. Parents often make their check-up calls between 6pm-8pm so not to disrupt their son or daughter's study time. They most certainly never call later than 10pm because they do not want to awaken them.

College students are quick learners!

Let me give it to you straight. The vast majority of students, at least those who are involved in social activities, more often than not start their evening out at 10pm or later. Many dances held on campus each week are pretty much deserted until 11pm or later. I recall the annual Homecoming Dance especially because the event was scheduled to close at 2am. Around 12:30am-1:00am, there would be a hundred students or more lined up to get inside. Please do not expect the students to call it an evening until the early hours. It is common to see hundreds of students mobile from 2:00-3:00am and later. Many remain awake through the night, especially on a Thursday night. A large number will skip classes on Friday, just to hang out at the dorm to rest so they can make the drive home for the weekend or prepare for yet another night out.

This does not mean that every student who participates in these late night outings is doing something bad. Many do not use drugs or alcohol, and most do not encounter problems with the campus police. It just happens to be a social norm on a college campus in this day and time. Believe me, you will find out if you try calling your son or daughter around 11pm some Thursday night. I'm telling you this too, so in case you ever were to call that late, you would not be alarmed if they were not in.

Like it or not, it happens.

CHAPTER 6

PROPPEDOPEN DOORS

Many times over the years, I found that crimes were committed in the residence halls simply because someone had propped open a door for convenience. Their goal was to allow themselves easy access when re-entering the residence hall. This can seem a very innocuous practice, and often results in nothing more than the intended convenience. However, criminals also appreciate the added convenience. Believe me; they will take full advantage of any opportunity given them.

Of course, college officials diligently warn students of this safety hazard as early as summer orientation sessions. Resident Assistants (R.A.s) also remind students to avoid this practice many times throughout the school year. Yet the innocent act of propping a door continues to occur, and so does crime.

I would encourage students to report instances of door propping to their R.A. so he/she can address this potentially dangerous issue with other residents. Hindsight is often 20/20, but in cases such as this, that clearer vision often comes at a steep price.

CHAPTER 7

WALKING ALONE

Regardless of the time of day, students should never walk alone in remote areas of a campus. In the late afternoon and evening hours, walking alone can have devastating effects. The following incident happened during the early years of my campus law enforcement career. To date, this case remains unsolved.

Exercise Wisely

Shannon, a fifteen-year-old non-student, lived near campus. She routinely walked alone, taking the road from her house, following it around the football stadium, and continuing on to an even more remote stretch of road. Unless there was a football game scheduled, the road circling the football stadium was seldom used.

Low man on the totem pole at the time, I usually found myself assigned to the second shift patrol. It was a known fact that I diligently patrolled the campus, often driving continuously for most of an eight-hour shift. I took the role of campus protector seriously. However, on this particular day, I called in sick with the flu. It could not have happened at a worse time for Shannon.

When Shannon failed to return home after her walk, her concerned parents called the campus and local police. Immediately, authorities organized a search for Shannon. By the next morning, hundreds of people had gathered to help search for her. Not a building or remote area on campus was left unchecked, but it was to no avail. Several days later, Shannon was discovered miles from campus severely beaten, raped, and left for dead.

Weeks passed before Shannon was able to sit through an interview and, even then, she proved to be a poor witness. Her attacker had repeatedly slammed her head against a wooden tool shed; this injury resulted in permanent brain damage that diluted her eyewitness testimony.

However, despite her injuries, Shannon was able to describe the initial attack. She reported seeing a disabled vehicle as she rounded the football stadium. A man stood nearby. As she approached, he attacked her from behind, striking her on the head with what she believed was a pistol. Her attacker then threw her into the vehicle's trunk and sped away.

Shannon, still conscious at that time, was able to describe several items she remembered seeing in the trunk. After a short drive, the car stopped. She was pulled from the trunk and dragged to an area behind a tool shed where she was raped and left for dead. I say she was left for dead because of the brutal manner in which she was beaten. Had her attacker known she was still alive, I am confident he would have continued the assault.

As I previously mentioned, this crime remained unsolved during my watch, and to this day, I feel guilty for calling in sick. That being said, there is little the campus police can do for students or visitors who fail to exercise caution and good judgment. A person, male or female, cannot walk alone in remote areas, regardless of the time of day.

CHAPTER 8

DANGEROUS FALLS

Sometimes events happen so quickly that the damage is done before anyone realizes a problem exists; by then it is too late to do anything but try to prevent future occurrences.

Party Pioneers

Ronnie and several of his dorm mates found the neatest place to party; a place where they could consume alcohol in excess, without fear of the campus police spoiling their fun. They enjoyed the privacy of this area on several occasions, and they were right in their assumption that campus police would not notice them. After all, until this event, campus police had no reason to look on top of the gymnasium for partying students.

One night Ronnie and his small group were on the rooftop and the beer was running low. Several students decided to climb down and bring back more beer. Later, when Ronnie's friends returned to the roof, Ronnie was nowhere to be found. After a short stay (long enough to consume a few more beers), the students climbed back down and returned to their residence hall for the night.

A few hours later, one of my police officers discovered Ronnie lying in a pool of blood at the base of the gymnasium. We learned later that he had waited for his friends to return, but when they failed to return quickly, Ronnie became worried and decided to find them. In the darkness (and his inebriated state), he missed the ladder attached to the gymnasium roof. Ronnie fell forty feet onto the sidewalk below. He survived the fall, but the last information I had was that he was still completely paralyzed from the fall.

Not all falls are the result of a student's wrongdoing. Some are simply unfortunate accidents, and no amount of pre-planning could prevent their occurrence.

Playing Tough

John was a first string football player and had one of the best personalities of any student I encountered over the years. He was always quick to offer a smile, or speak with me whenever I had occasion to see him on campus.

During a football game early in the season, John suffered an injury that at the time did not appear to be serious. Players laughed, commenting, "He got his bell rung!" After the team doctor cleared him to return to the game, he did. John did not complain the remainder of the game, or any other time during the last few weeks of the season.

Shortly after the football season ended, we had a light snow. Snow was rare in this particular area, so students went outside to enjoy the activities in full, including snowball fights. John found himself actively involved in one when he slipped and fell in the freshly fallen snow.

After falling, John immediately felt a tingling sensation in his legs, and was slow to get up. Being the tough football player that he was, John walked the injury off, and returned to his residence hall for the evening. As his dorm room was located on the third level, he also climbed three flights of stairs before reaching his room.

While trying to undress for bed, John suddenly felt numbness in his legs. Worried, he called the campus police for help. An officer arrived to the room; he immediately called for an ambulance. John mentioned that the numbness had left his legs and he believed he could walk downstairs to meet the paramedics. The officer and John walked down the three flights of stairs, and waited for the ambulance to arrive.

John never walked again.

We learned later that the football injury resulted in a cracked vertebrate that, left untreated, resulted in a severed spinal cord when John fell in the snow.

I often wonder had the officer forced John to remain in his room and wait for medical help to immobilize him, rather than walk down the stairs that night, would he still have use of his legs. Unfortunately, we will never know the answer to that, and I am sure the officer involved will likely never stop questioning his decision that night.

In retrospect, the gymnasium roof is no longer accessible to students, and there were policies implemented within the departments I managed regarding safe transport of injured students. However, despite best intentions, there will always be some incident the campus police will be ill equipped to handle. As I stated earlier, hindsight is usually 20/20, but it is still hindsight.

CHAPTER 9

FRESHMEN AND VEHICLES

Allowing, or not allowing, freshmen students to have vehicles on campus has always been a highly debatable issue for most college campuses. I honestly cannot tell you who is right in this ongoing argument.

Students are different in so many ways. Although they are all essentially adults, some come to campus much more mature, and perceptive to the world around them. However, some come to campus oblivious to the cruelties that can occur. These latter students might benefit from restrictions on possessing a vehicle at the beginning of the school year. I have always thought freshmen should wait to bring a vehicle to campus until after fall break, at the earliest. Bottom line, parents and their student have to reach a decision and make the most of it.

Be aware that some colleges and universities make this decision for you. Many higher learning institutions do not allow freshmen to have vehicles on campus, and even when they do, freshmen might be restricted to remote parking lots or not driving on campus except during weekends or breaks.

CHAPTER 10

LOANING VEHICLES TO OTHER STUDENTS

I learned over the years, after countless interviews with parents and students, some students will never learn to say "no" when someone asks to borrow their car. In their defense, I will add that peer pressure is rampant on college campuses. Students who want to fit in at any cost may understandably succumb to the pressure of being asked repeatedly for use of their vehicle.

Comments I seemed to hear with regular occurrence was, "He seemed like a pretty cool guy," or "He lived on my hall and I figured he was cool." These victims thought they were good judges of character, when most times they only knew the offender for minutes, hours, or days at the most.

Johnny's Joyride

Jennifer went to an off-campus party one Friday evening, and immediately hit it off with Johnny. He was handsome, with a quick smile and great personality—and he was not drinking like most of the other partygoers. Jennifer knew that Johnny was going to be someone special. As it turns out, Johnny was very special indeed.

After talking for an hour or so, Johnny asked to borrow Jennifer's vehicle so he could run to the store. Thinking he was one of the "good guys", she readily agreed. He made mention that he would be back "as soon as possible". Two things he failed to explain to Jennifer were "as soon as possible" could be just about any length of time and the "store" was located two-hundred miles away.

When Johnny did not return that night, or the next, Jennifer began to worry. It was late Sunday evening when she received a telephone call from Johnny, asking if she would come bail him out of jail. Did I mention he called from another state entirely? Apparently, Johnny became intoxicated and, after a high-speed chase with the police, crashed Jennifer's vehicle. He mentioned that if she could contact his parents, they would help pay for the damages to her vehicle.

When Jennifer came to my office and reported the incident, I advised her that I would help, if possible. I warned her, with the person being in jail, and out of state, it might be difficult at best. She gave me the phone number Johnny had provided her with to contact his parents, and I agreed to make the call.

A male voice answered my call, and after I explained who I was and the reason for the call, he gave a stern reply. He advised me that Johnny was a stepson, who had caused nothing but problems over the years and that he was sick and tired of bailing the jerk out! Not the resolution I had hoped for, but not entirely unexpected either.

Jennifer finally recovered her losses, but it took much time and effort on her part, and I am sure her insurance rates went up significantly as a result! I knew her for the remainder of her college career, and eventually she was able to smile when the subject of loaning her car came up. To this day, I would imagine she never hands over her car keys to anyone!

Wrongly Accused

Thomas was a freshman football player with much promise. Not only was he touted as an exceptional football player, he was an even better student. Understandably, I was surprised when the local police came to my office one morning and reported that Thomas' vehicle had been identified in an armed robbery the night before.

Officers brought Thomas to my office for questioning, where I promptly read his Miranda Rights. It was clear he was confused and highly alarmed. This was his first brush with the police, and he did not know what to think. He also had no clue why officers had come to his room and escorted him to my office.

I learned that while Thomas and several friends were playing cards in his dorm room the night before, a student named Joe (who also lived in the dorm) walked in and asked to borrow Thomas' vehicle to make a run to the local convenience store for snacks. Without hesitation, Thomas tossed the keys to a student he later described as "a cool dude who lived on his hall". The two had only just met earlier that week.

It was the second week of school and Thomas believed himself to be, as all students do, a good judge of character. Joe was cool. Joe seemed friendly. What else did he need to know about the guy? Thomas stated that his new "friend" Joe returned the keys to him a short time later. Joe even thanked Thomas for letting him use the car. What Joe failed to mention was that while he had Thomas's vehicle, he also attempted to rob the store.

With friends like that . . . . well, you know the saying as well as I do.

I could go on and on with horror stories involving loaned vehicles, but it would be of little use. I even thought stamping the message into the foreheads of all incoming freshmen might help, but I soon dismissed that idea. Know that campus police will be putting out the message at orientations and throughout the school year. Heed their warnings. Just say "no" when someone asks to borrow your vehicle! There is no need to make excuses for not loaning a vehicle. Simply say "no".

CHAPTER 11

BATTERIES, FLATS, AND VEHICLE MAINTENANCE

I t might be difficult to believe, but students who have vehicles on campus do not necessarily drive them all of the time. Many students find they have limited free time due to classes, class assignments, and/ or work obligations. Some may have financial limitations that prevent them from driving too much ($4/gallon gas, anyone?). Others discover there are simply so many activities available on campus that using the car on a daily basis is not as important as their having one *just in case*.

A large percentage of students come to school thinking they cannot live without their vehicle. Within weeks, they park their vehicle and leave them sitting for extended periods. I have known students who drive to campus at the beginning of the semester, park their vehicle, and do not return to it until fall break, Thanksgiving, or even Christmas.

When a vehicle is unattended for long periods, tires can lose air pressure and batteries can lose their charge, to the point where the vehicle will not crank. There are also instances where vandals may have damaged a vehicle. Should this be the case, students who fail to check on their car periodically cannot provide the campus police with an accurate time-line, making it more difficult to solve the crime.

My officers were trained to be proactive when patrolling the campus. This involved looking for signs that a vehicle had been left unattended for long periods. If they suspected this, they were instructed to contact those owners to determine if there was a problem with the vehicle. This was extremely important in the days immediately preceding school breaks or holidays.

Under my watch, messages were posted throughout the residence halls asking students to check on their vehicles prior to the last day of class. I did this so if they encountered a problem, repairs could be made prior to the start of break. Unfortunately, it was all too common to find students stranded on campus during breaks simply because they had not checked on their vehicles in advance to resolve some inexpensive repair.

Note to parents: you should also know that I have seen students use the *emergency repair* excuse to remain on campus during break periods. Parents expect their son or daughter to be excited about coming home during breaks and holidays; however, some students adapt to college life so well, and they develop such good friendships on campus, they actually prefer staying on campus even when classes are not in session. In my opinion, this can be a sign that the student is maturing and preparing to move out into the "real world". Sometimes though, there is another side to the thought process; for instance, the behavior that has become the norm on campus might not be well received at home.

For legitimate issues, I made it a policy to keep tools, air tanks, and fix-a-flat repair canisters in all patrol vehicles. This way, if a student encountered minor issues, officers could help get them easily and safely to a nearby service station for professional repairs.

When vehicles are parked for extended periods, students not only encounter problems with tires, belts that become loose, and so forth, they also forget to perform regular maintenance on the vehicle (oil changes, tire rotation, and ensuring that fluid levels are replenished). This is often the first time a student is responsible for maintaining a vehicle without the mother and/or father's attention to detail. It is good practice to remind your student of routine maintenance until it becomes a habit for them to do this themselves. If an ounce of prevention is worth a pound of cure, so is checking your vehicle on a regular basis.

PART TWO

CRIME ON CAMPUS

CHAPTER 12

CAMPUS VIOLATIONS AND CRIMINAL CHARGES

W henever students enroll in a college or university, they will receive a student handbook. The handbook, often called the student's "bible", contains the rules and regulations students must adhere to while on campus. Penalties for violations are also noted. Parents and students should study this book well.

Too often, incoming freshmen fail to read the institution's rules and regulations, choosing instead to listen to upperclassmen. Nine times out of ten, when a student finds himself/herself in trouble, one of the first comments to come forth is that an upperclassman told them their behavior was acceptable.

Students are also expected to adhere to state and local laws, many of which they might not know exist. This can be especially confusing for out-of-state students who are familiar with a different set of regulatory rules, as local laws often vary from state to state.

It is important to note that whenever a student commits a violation of state and local law, he or she could also be arrested and charged on a campus judiciary level for the same offense. Although argued by some that this is a form of double jeopardy, it is important to know this argument has been widely unsuccessful. Read the student handbook; there will more than likely be a notation that students can be charged both ways for the same offense. For example, if a student is arrested off-campus for possession of drugs with the intent to sell and deliver, he or she stands a good chance of being charged on a campus level for conduct unbecoming a student. If a student is arrested off-campus for assault, he/she may also face charges on a campus level for the same offense. A conviction in court does not necessarily effect what happens on the campus and vice versa. There are times when a student might have criminal charges dismissed, yet still receive penalties on campus.

Often, college/university officials differ in their opinions on how to handle situations that occur both on and off campus. Naturally, officials in the student affairs office are the strongest advocates for students, and will often make every effort to handle problems on a campus judiciary level in order to retain that student. In contrast, the campus police may view violations from a different perspective, and typically promote stricter campus penalties, arrest, or both.

Parents can also have an impact on the outcome of campus judiciary proceedings, considering they are often the one paying tuition; remember, most colleges and universities depend on revenues from enrollment. I observed many situations where I was confident a student facing disciplinary charges would receive suspension, only to see a concerned parent appear on the scene and sway the outcome. Granted, no amount of parental pressure can alter the final judgment in some offenses. In these cases, students are sent home.

That being said, it never bothered me when parents voiced their concerns. In fact, I encouraged parents to become involved when their son or daughter faced difficulties. This can often be the most important action you take when problems arise.

Peeping Tom . . . or Burt, in This Case

Jan lived in a female residence hall located on the west end of campus. While taking a shower late one evening, she noticed a male student peering at her from beneath the shower curtain. Startled, she screamed and he ran from the bathroom.

When officers arrived on the scene, Jan stated she could identify the male because he happened to be in her biology class. His name was Burt. It was simply good fortune that another off-duty officer happened to be in the area just moments prior to the incident. He also confirmed seeing Burt and another male hanging around the female residence hall.

The following morning, I interviewed the male believed to have been with Burt, hoping he might offer a statement to corroborate the information I had already received. The male admitted entering the residence hall with Burt. He told me as they walked down the hallway, they could hear a shower running. He explained that after Burt entered the bathroom, he chickened-out and ran from the building. Minutes later, Burt came running through the door laughing, and they both ran from the area. Burt never told him what happened inside the bathroom. I did.

Later, as I interviewed Burt, he denied being in the residence hall altogether. However, in the process of denying his involvement, he hung his head saying, "My parents are going to be upset with me."

I stated the obvious, "Burt, if you didn't do anything wrong, why are your parents going to be upset?"

He refused to answer the question. Based on statements from witnesses, and the victim, I charged Burt on a campus level only. The victim stated that she would be satisfied if he only faced campus judiciary charges, so I did not pursue formal criminal charges against Burt. It would become one of the few times in nearly thirty years that I would second-guess my actions. I knew Burt was guilty, but his parents arrived on the date of his campus hearing and caused such uproar that the campus court dismissed the charges against him. The campus court was intimidated by the actions of the parents.

I spoke with the father afterward and let him know that, while I respected his defense of his son, at some point he needed to realize that Burt had in fact broken the law. Not only did he break the law, but he also violated the safety of another individual. The father agreed, and then left the building. He never argued; he knew Burt was guilty too.

In Burt's defense, he remained on campus and graduated as expected. He never committed another reported offense. However, one can easily see how this situation could escalate given that he received little more than a slap on the hand for his actions against Jan.

Housekeeping Blues

Sue was a housekeeping employee assigned to one of the male residence halls. She often chose to clean bathrooms during the mid-morning hours when most students were in class. Sue always propped open the bathroom door and placed a sign in the doorway to alert residents that she was inside cleaning. That practice seemed sufficient until a student named Barney Slocumb walked in one morning.

Sue reported to our officers that while she was cleaning one of the urinals, Barney walked over to the adjacent urinal and, with her standing there, relieved himself. Sue calmly walked out and called the campus police.

I summoned Barney to my office. When he arrived, I took a moment to study the young man. He was a large, brawny fellow, and judging from the arrogant way he stared back at me, I could tell he more than likely had been the bullying type as an adolescent. For his interview, I chose to veer from the typical Miranda Rights introduction. I explained to Barney that I was not going to read his rights.

I did, however, look across my desk at the young man and calmly say, "Barney, I have a dilemma, and I need your help."

He looked at me, puzzled. I waited for a moment as his face reddened in irritation.

I continued, "You see, I need to determine whether you're a sexual predator who needs to be arrested and expelled immediately or if you are you just a rude son-of-a-bitch who made a poor decision." I shuffled some papers on my desk, "You have ten seconds to answer my question."

Barney stared at me for a brief moment before lowering his head, "I'm just a rude son-of-a-bitch, sir."

I rapped my knuckles on the desk and said, "Well, at least you're smart enough to know *that* much."

I could have dealt with Barney in a number of different ways. I could have told him from the beginning that Sue was content with only pressing campus judiciary charges. I could have read him his rights and arrested him for indecent exposure. However, Barney left my office that day and made every effort to clean up his act. I never had another problem out of him. Barney graduated and went on to become a productive member of society.

CHAPTER 13

PARKING PERMITS AND TICKETS

Parking permits and decals are unavoidable on a college/university campus, as this system provides the campus police with the means to identify vehicles on campus. Parking decals help to determine if the vehicles are parked in the correct assigned parking area, and to determine the vehicle does, in fact, belong on campus.

Naturally, not all vehicles driving and or operating on campus will belong to faculty, staff and students. There are many legitimate visitors to a campus on any given day. However, campus police must be able to identify those who are not on the campus for legitimate reasons. Many persons find a college/university campus an attractive place to visit, especially during the opening weeks of each semester. During those weeks, the campus is home to a new class of students, many of who are naïve to the criminal elements that frequent a campus.

The price of permits and tickets varies a great deal from campus to campus. I am not sure those who charge extremely high fees or issue costly fines can justify the amounts affixed to either, but ask during an orientation session to see if you can come away with a good answer.

Unfortunately, an issue parents find out about far too late is that students will likely receive a ticket at some point during their collegiate careers. Most campuses employ aggressive traffic enforcement techniques due to space limitations, and there are frequent struggles between different factions on campus who are vying for close, convenient parking spaces. There might be the occasional aggressive parking officer or administrator who looks upon tickets as a source of revenue for the college/university, but with any luck, you will not encounter that.

The competition for close, convenient parking on campuses is keen. Faculty demand close, convenient parking because they feel it is within their rights. Resident students demand close, convenient parking to their living quarters, and use safety as a valid reasoning and bargaining tool. Many times commuters find they are on the lower end of the spectrum when it comes to close, convenient spaces because they are on campus the least amount of time. Some schools leave parking enforcement to the campus police, while others (which I highly recommend) create traffic and parking committees consisting of faculty, staff, and students that are responsible for developing rules and regulations.

I could not begin to tell you how many times parents would tell me, after learning their son or daughter had accumulated three to four-hundred dollars in parking fines, that they had given the student money to buy a permit at the first of the semester, only to learn later the student spent the money on something else. It happens often; trust me. Make sure the permit is purchased and visible at all times to avoid the inevitable hassle and monetary troubles.

No Extra Perks

Cindy was a very popular student on campus. Between her role as cheerleader and full-time student, Cindy's free time was extremely limited. This is the explanation she offered for violating parking rules, and incurring several hundred dollars in fines. As a commuter, she did not have time to park in a remote parking lot and walk to classes, so she parked in faculty/staff spaces instead.

I can still recall the day she walked into the police department wearing a rather short mini-skirt. Cindy walked into my office, hopped up on the desk, and asked if I might help her by reducing the ticket fines. I suggested that she first needed to get off my desk and have a seat in one of the nearby chairs. With a sudden redness to her cheeks, she climbed down and took a seat. I told her that had she come into my office in a professional manner, I would have made an effort to help. Since she acted in such a disrespectful way, however, I would not reduce any of the fines.

She left in a tiff, paid the fines, and best I can recall, she never received any more parking tickets.

Girl Trouble

Tom was a freshman football player, and well liked throughout campus because he was so easy going. He was a student who was sure to spend his entire college career without encountering a problem. Knowing him to be this way, I was puzzled when I found out Tom had accumulated about three-hundred dollars in parking tickets.

When I called him to the office to talk about it, he was puzzled as well. Tom stated he always parked in his assigned lot, and that he had never received a ticket. When I produced copies of the tickets charged to his account, and where the violations occurred, he quickly realized what happened. Tom would occasionally let his girlfriend borrow his car. It was determined that she was the violator.

When she arrived at the office and I confronted her with the facts, she admitted to the violations. She explained that she simply tossed the tickets into the trash each time, thinking that since it was not her car, she could not be held accountable. Tom paid the tickets, and I doubt that his girlfriend reimbursed him.

Students might be able to withstand peer pressure from friends when asked to borrow their car, but I am not sure any amount of preaching will persuade a student to say "no" to a boyfriend or girlfriend. I hope when they do loan a vehicle under these circumstances, they will fare better than Tom.

In short, parking enforcement is unavoidable. Those who violate the rules and regulations must be held accountable. I never agreed with allowing anyone (faculty, staff, or student) to accumulate excessive amounts. I began a policy, towards the later part of my career, to prevent this from happening. If an individual received more than three tickets in one semester, a letter was issued to that individual reminding them of the rules and regulations, and alerting them to the fact that further violations would result in their loss of driving privileges on campus. The offender was required to sign off on the letter, acknowledging that he or she had been warned. Future violations resulted in the immediate towing of their vehicle and loss of driving privileges on campus for one year. This might seem harsh, but it worked. Those who were chronic violators stopped parking improperly and did not receive additional tickets.

Problem solved.

CHAPTER 14

DRUGS AND ALCOHOL

As previously mentioned, I spent the first sixteen years of my campus law enforcement career at a private, 4-year liberal arts college where campus rules prohibited the use and possession of drugs and alcohol. This did not mean that these substances were not present in quantities, because they were. It did mean, however, that students made great efforts to conceal their use of prohibited items because being caught possessing, or under the influence, of these substances could bring disastrous results. The fines and penalties ranged from monetary fines, arrests, and even suspension. Students with more than one campus disciplinary action and/ or misdemeanor arrests faced harsher disciplinary measures than first-time offenders.

When I first arrived at the state-funded university, it was the exact opposite. There, it was not against university rules for students, aged twenty-one and over, to possess and use alcohol on campus. Students could possess as much as two cases of beer in their room, without being in violation of campus policy. This always seemed a bit excessive to me. Drugs, while prohibited on this campus, were still present in significant quantities.

Be aware that when your son or daughter moves in at the beginning of the semester, they will encounter opportunities to experiment with drugs and alcohol. Their new roommate may participate in some form of substance abuse; someone down the hall surely will; and, someone within the dormitory will definitely have serious problems with drugs, alcohol, or both. Talk with your student well in advance. Remind them that it is okay to say, "no." I realize that might sound a bit corny, but many students do refrain from using drugs and alcohol during their collegiate career.

During orientation sessions, I made sure to take the opportunity to ask students to make anonymous calls when someone in their dorm is involved with drugs, whether it is simple use, or distribution, because problems often result from condoning such behavior. I always believed that many dorm thefts, which I will talk about later, often occurred because of drugs or alcohol. I will share some of these stories later within this book.

I also asked for anonymous reports because I did not need to know the identity of the person reporting a problem. A small percentage of the student population has serious problems with drugs or alcohol, but that small percentage is responsible for a large percentage of problems on campus. Many students I encountered over the years claimed they had used drugs and/or alcohol since adolescence; a few commented that it was a family tradition. One student I arrested for possession of marijuana with intent to sell and distribute told me his parents would not be upset with him. Apparently, they had smoked together since his pre-teen years, and it was a way of life for them, just as they also expected to encounter problems with police from time to time. I never met this student's parents, so the story he told was never confirmed, but I had no reason to doubt him either. He was as matter-of-fact about being arrested as you might be for getting an overdue book fine from the library.

Make sure the campus you choose admits that drugs and alcohol are present, and that both are concerns that are addressed on campus. This does not necessarily mean students have to be arrested for violating the rules, regulations, and criminal statutes, but the college or university must take a proactive approach, with education and enforcement in mind.

At the state funded university where I ended my career, the university actually had a written agreement with the local district attorney's office that would allow students to be charged for first offense misdemeanors involving drugs and alcohol on a campus judiciary level. This was because the campus penalties were more severe than what the courts would have handed out. It also prevented the courts from being further bogged down due to our aggressive enforcement on the campus.

The Clery Act, discussed earlier, requires colleges and universities to publish campus crime statistics, including campus disciplinary charges involving drugs and or alcohol. Do all of the schools report statistics accurately? I cannot answer that. I can tell you I always reported the crimes/campus disciplinary actions that occurred at the schools where I worked. I always thought it best to disclose this information and let the campus community know that crime does occur, but I also used the opportunity to discuss the many things the campus police were doing to *prevent* similar events from occurring in the future, or to prevent crimes altogether.

When you are considering a college or university for your child, look at the crime/campus disciplinary statistics they publish. If you discover the campus did not report any alcohol arrests, look to see if they, in fact, charged a large number of students on a campus level with the offense. It might be that the school had an arrangement similar to that I described earlier, wherein the district attorney's office accepted campus judiciary penalties rather than clog the courts with students. If a campus does not list arrest or campus judiciary charges for drug and alcohol misdemeanors, I would suggest the student body is one of the best mannered in the country, or that the administration and campus police are not enforcing rules and regulations, as they should. As I have already mentioned, a campus is not unlike the community in which you live, drugs and alcohol are present.

CHAPTER 15

STEROIDS

Colleges and universities are constantly seeking ways to provide entertainment for the students and the campus community. We had one such event, professional wrestling, that I wished had never been scheduled.

A Different Reaction

Joe and Tom were two aspiring athletes. Thoughts of playing professional football were not beyond either student's realm of possibilities. Both were well over six feet tall and very muscular, but after watching the professional wrestlers appear on campus, the two students decided that wrestling was the sport for them.

It was also readily apparent to both of these students that they were not nearly as large as the wrestlers they had observed. The boys knew that in order to compete they had to bulk up significantly. Within very little time, they were able to locate a company that provided steroids through the mail, and they placed an order.

When the product arrived, each gave the other an injection, and then waited to see the results. Joe felt fine, with no side effects at all. With Tom, the results were far different. Within minutes of the injection, he felt odd; within a few hours, he thought he was coming down with the flu.

Tom chose to lie down and rest. He remained in bed through the evening. Joe checked on his friend before bedtime, and though Tom was still feeling poorly, he told Joe he would be okay after he rested for the night.

Tom never woke up.

The following morning our officers responded to the room after receiving a 911 call. Tom breathed his last breath as officers arrived.

An autopsy revealed that while the steroids did not kill him, they contributed to his death. Tom had a problem with a heart valve that neither he nor his family were aware of, and the steroid added to his system was too much for his heart condition.

Students are going to experiment with drugs and alcohol, and other things. Experimentation is part of the learning process and something we cannot prevent. I hope that those who read this story make a better decision when it comes their turn to face something new.

CHAPTER 16

DATE RAPE

I do not use the term "date rape" when speaking with the campus community. When a girl says "No", the offense is a crime, and that crime is rape, pure and simple. I cannot tell you the actual number of rapes reported during my tenure as a campus police officer. However, I can tell you the exact number of rapes that led to criminal prosecution—none.

How could this happen? One possibility is the aversion to negative publicity. I have known university officials who would stop at nothing to prevent negative publicity. This often creates conflict between campus police and administration. It was always my stance to treat each reported rape as a crime, investigate it as such, and then allow the criminal justice system to resolve the matter. At the same time, there were key administrators who would speak with the victim, hoping to persuade them to handle the matter on a campus judiciary level.

Was this behavior ethical? I am not sure I can answer that, but if justice is served and the victim is okay with the outcome, I am not sure it matters. I do know I never felt good about handling the matter on a campus judiciary level unless the court system made it known that the case was not prosecutable.

A Party to Forget

Melanie attended an off-campus party with a group of girlfriends. It was a Thursday night, which on a college campus is the unofficial party night. Sometime after midnight, Melanie's friends decided to return to campus, but Melanie told them that she would catch a ride back with John, a person she met earlier that night.

Melanie did not seem intoxicated, so the friends left, unconcerned. Later, after several more drinks, John drove Melanie back to her residence hall and offered to walk her to her room. After they entered the room, Melanie said they kissed for a minute and then they both undressed. Moments later John was trying to force himself on her, and Melanie struggled, telling him, "No."

She did not report screaming for help, only struggling to make John stop. She was unable to do so and he committed the rape, dressed, and left the room. Rather than report the rape to campus police, Melanie dressed and walked across campus to her boyfriend's residence where they had consensual sex. She felt guilty about what had taken place with John and wanted to reinforce her affection towards her boyfriend.

Approximately twelve hours after John raped her, Melanie reported the crime to campus police. It was impossible to collect evidence, and even then, when the district attorney was provided the facts of the case, they refused to try the case. Fortunately, we were able to charge John on a campus judiciary level and he was suspended immediately. Melanie, like so many other victims of this crime, dropped out of school shortly afterward.

Hear No Evil

Mary, a hearing and verbally impaired student, lived alone in her dorm room on campus. She preferred it that way. Other girls did not want to stay with her because she slept with her door unlocked at night. Mary was not a careless or naive girl. No, she was afraid that a fire alarm might sound, and since she could not hear it, there was a chance no one would be able to get into her room to rescue her.

Within a few weeks of arriving on campus, Mary met a freshman boy named John. Mary and John made an immediate connection, and could often be seen sitting behind the student center after the evening meal, exchanging notes. In one note, Mary agreed to allow John to come visit her after hours, telling him she would meet him at the rear door around midnight so he could sneak into the dorm without being noticed.

Later that night, Mary changed her mind and decided against meeting John. She could not call and tell John this, because she was unable to use a telephone due to her impairment. John arrived at the dormitory at the scheduled time, and found a rear door propped open. Mary was not there, but he figured she had left it that way for him, so he continued down the hall to her room. There he found Mary's door unlocked, continued inside, undressed, and climbed into bed with her.

Within moments, John was on top of Mary, forcing himself upon her. Mary was barely awake by the time the act was taking place and could not prevent it. She struggled, trying to stop John, but could not. Mary tried to scream for help, but no sound came out.

What John did not realize, was that shortly before midnight, two female residents in the dormitory decided to make a late-night run to a local convenience store and get a snack. They propped open the exit door so they could get back into the dormitory without having to walk all the way to the other side of the building.

When provided the facts of the case, and the colorful notes that John provided on his behalf, the district attorney decided it was not a case they could prosecute. The college found John guilty on a campus judiciary level; his punishment was suspension. Like Melanie, Mary dropped out of school shortly thereafter.

I could spend four chapters on rape alone.

Unfortunately, this crime shows no sign of stopping on college campuses nationwide. During orientation sessions, students receive information about rape. It boils down to this:

- When you attend parties with friends, leave with friends.
- While at a party, do not drink from open containers that someone else provides, or mixed drinks that are available.
- "No" means no—failure to stop at this point is a crime, plain and simple.

CHAPTER 17

SEXUAL HARASSMENT

While this offense might not carry the same weight in the public's eye as rape, the victims of sexual harassment are no less affected by the offender's actions. Usually when a victim reports this crime, the first thought in many peoples' minds and often my own, was could it possibly be true? The offender oftentimes seemed the least likely to commit such a crime. I learned, after years of experience, to listen to the victim. When the victim would attribute an action or comment the offender supposedly made, and if it seemed far-fetched, it was usually a fact to reply upon. I will give you a few examples of what I mean in the following pages.

Not So Funny Business

Clare was a female housekeeping employee, assigned to the second-shift. Her normal hours were 3pm-11pm, and the vast majority of the time, those who worked on her shift were assigned to two—to three-person crews. The work assignments varied each day, but the crews always worked together.

When Clare came to my office one afternoon, and began telling me about how her supervisor exposed himself to her the night before at work, I listened. She told me the supervisor had assigned her to work in a remote location, alone. This caught my attention, because as I said earlier, second-shift crews typically worked in teams. She continued, saying that shortly after she began working, the supervisor came into the room, lowered his pants, and exposed himself. She also stated that while he was exposed he said, "I'm bad, I'm bad!"

Based on her statements, and other facts considered, this incident was remedied quickly to her satisfaction.

Touch-Me-Not

A female employee working in the campus police department walked into my office one afternoon and informed me that Roger had touched her inappropriately. When asked what results she wanted, she said she only wanted the inappropriate action to stop. I spoke with Roger and, although his version differed completely, I advised him that any unwanted touching was considered an offense. He assured me there would not be any further complaints lodged against him by this female.

As always, when a complaint was filed, I wrote a detailed report and forwarded the information to my supervisor. With this incident, since it involved people working in my department, I also had a conversation with my supervisor to make sure I had covered all bases in case the behavior was reported again.

Several years after leaving this campus, I received a call from a female employee at the college, Sarah. She told me that Roger had touched her inappropriately, and had done the same with a number of other females on campus. She filed a complaint with Equal Employment Opportunity Commission (EEOC). The college's response to the complaint was that this was the first time Roger's behavior had been brought to anyone's attention. I advised her that a report had been filed several years ago, and that I had even spoken with a senior administrator about the complaint. I shared this with the EEOC investigators, but since I was not directly involved, I never learned the outcome. Suffice to say that Roger, who by that time held a high-level position, is no longer employed at the college.

Incidents such as these happen in workplaces across the country every day. I would venture to say that the majority are never reported. Even in Roger's case, many of the females did not come forward until one of his alleged victims filed the EEOC complaint. Know that the campus police are there to help all those who work and live on the campus, but victims have to come forward in order for an investigation and solution to occur. A proactive campus police department should provide opportunities to educate the campus community about harassment and how to report it.

CHAPTER 18

HAZING

Whenever hazing occurs, colleges or universities often handle the matter on a campus judiciary level rather than prosecute the offenders through the criminal court system. I lost many an argument with administrators on this issue, as too many times I thought the penalties doled out did not fit the crime. A conviction of hazing in the criminal courts required that the offender be expelled from school, which usually did not occur when the offender was found responsible of a campus violation only.

Hazing usually occurs in fraternities and sororities. It can also happen within the many athletic arenas, in classrooms, and in the residence halls. The key is for students to realize the difference between good-natured ribbing and hazing. Something intended to be good-natured does not place another person in harm's way, nor does it continue over extended periods. Bottom line, if an event is not fun for everyone involved, it is not fun at all.

Some students want to fit in so badly, they will allow themselves to be ridiculed, or even endure hardships, pain, and suffering. I hope these students will eventually learn that those who place others in harm's way, or those who subject others to pain and suffering, is not someone worth looking up to. Rather, be an individual, and people will want to join you.

William's Revenge

William was timid, of slight build, and very much an introvert. He did not make any friends in the first two or three weeks of his freshmen semester; if anything, he did just the opposite. Though he never officially reported the abuse he endured, I later learned that many guys living in his dorm ridiculed him on multiple occasions. While there was never any physical abuse (his aggressors preferred to taunt or bait him), he nevertheless suffered from these forms of intimidation. It was not unusual for his sleep to be disturbed by his assailants taunting, and he was often ridiculed in the cafeteria in front of others. William's suffering only worsened as the semester progressed.

I received a report one afternoon that someone had smeared human excrement throughout one of the freshman dorms. It happened to be the dorm where William lived. When I arrived on the scene, students were in an uproar. The foul smelling material had been smeared on doors, doorknobs, pay telephones in the hallways, bathroom mirrors, and anywhere else you could imagine. A complete and thorough washing of all the surfaces with bleach was required, and still I wondered about the safety of the residents.

Upon interviewing people in the dorm, I learned that William had been seen carrying a large tin bucket down the hallway the night before. I went to his room to talk with him and he confessed almost immediately to the malicious act. He proceeded to tell me of the abuse he had suffered for weeks, and that he simply could not take it any longer, so he fought back in his own way.

Had William reported the initial hazing, it would have stopped abruptly. In his defense, during those early years of campus law enforcement, we did not take opportunities to speak with incoming freshmen and warn them of dangers that might await them. We did not make it known to them that reporting was the best method of addressing and stopping abuse. Had we addressed this issue back then with incoming freshmen, this unfortunate incident might never have happened.

William never provided me with the names of those who had treated him so badly so I was not able to charge anyone with hazing. William found them guilty and enacted punishment suitable for the crimes, at least in his mind. Because of his actions, William was permanently expelled from this particular school.

Handcuffed

Fred was a typical freshman, eighteen years old, with boyish looks and brilliant red hair. The bullies in the dorm took particular enjoyment in making fun of Fred's hair and, although Fred found himself ridiculed frequently, he never reported the incidents. He figured it would stop eventually. It did.

While on patrol late one night, as I neared the outdoor tennis courts, I noticed that the lights were on. I had turned them off around midnight. Less than thirty minutes later, someone was evidently playing tennis. As I approached the courts, a group of girls left the area, laughing loudly as they ran from the area. I knew something was amiss and I soon realized what it was. There stood Fred, handcuffed to the tennis court's perimeter fence, naked from head to toe.

Some of the bullies in Fred's dorm took the opportunity to strip Fred of his clothes, handcuff him to the fence, and then telephone the girls dorm to invite onlookers. As troubling as it was that the bullies did this, it was even more difficult to believe that a large number of girls responded to the scene, and yet none of them reported the incident.

Fred was freed from the plight that he was in and transported to his room. Even after much coaxing, he never identified those who were responsible. He dropped out of school the following day. Yet again, the hazers went unpunished.

Flagpole

Bobby was another typical freshman who badly wanted to fit in with the cool guys in his residence hall. Unfortunately, from the first days of the semester he was picked on and taunted by the bullies in his residence hall. It was no surprise that he accepted an invitation from the guys one night for him to join them as they "rolled" the campus. It was a long-standing tradition to roll the campus with toilet paper the night before a football game and Bobby was thrilled to have a part in this big event.

Bobby soon found that he was, once again, the target of ridicule. His "friends" stripped him down to his underwear and bound him to the rope that was attached to the flagpole in the center of the campus. Once attached to the rope, he was hoisted a few feet off the ground and left there for onlookers to view. Many came by that evening, but no one offered to help him down or even call the campus police to report what they witnessed.

Bobby was eventually released when one of our officers noticed him attached to the flagpole, but he would not provide the names of those who had committed this crime against him. The following day Bobby packed his belongings and left campus.

Students need to report bad behavior quickly, and not allow it to escalate. When the bullies of the world, and every campus has them, are allowed to operate full throttle, the results can be devastating. Reporting these individuals to the campus police, or even residence life staff members, will most often result in an immediate change in the behavior without future harm coming to the victim. As a last resort, a victim might consider making an anonymous complaint to the campus police, and allow them to sort out whether a crime is being committed or not.

See No Evil

Billy was one of the blind students on campus. I was never able to determine if he was a victim of hazing or not. I honestly think he believed he was invited to do wild and crazy things with the guys because he was a part of the in-crowd; however, I think the people he considered friends were having fun at his expense more often than not. Regardless, I was never able to charge any of his fellow students with hazing because he never reported it.

Even when asked, Billy denied any wrongdoing on anyone's part. You might be able to decide after reading the following, or at least it might give you an idea what your son or daughter may expect when they arrive on campus if they have a disability. Sometimes they are accepted by other students, sometimes not, just like any other student when they first arrive on campus. All too often, innocent fun turns into something grave.

I was in my office one day when the head professional at one of the local golf courses called to report an incident that just happened. Seems three of our students had been at the golf course shortly before, and one of them drove the golf cart across several greens, into sand traps, and even crashed the cart into a tree. The pro provided me with the names of those involved, including the name of the student who had signed for the cart as the responsible driver. The driver was Billy. It seems that several of Billy's friends invited him to join them for a round of golf, and allowed him to drive the cart on voice commands they offered. They were not welcomed back to the course, although they managed to avoid paying restitution for damages. Upon learning that Billy had signed for the cart (while wearing sunglasses to hide his blindness), I believe the golf pro was too embarrassed to pursue charges against Billy and his friends.

This was not the only incident involving Billy.

I always employed eight to ten students to help with parking control whenever we had ballgames or special events on campus. Students who directed traffic were required to wear a safety vest and carry a flashlight so motorists could see them easily. I drove into one of the parking lots one evening to check on the traffic, and there stood Billy, smack dab in the middle of the parking lot, wearing a vest, waving a flashlight, and directing traffic.

Several of his friends had discovered the extra vests and flashlights that were on hand for regular members of the parking crew, and had supplied Billy accordingly, assigning him a spot with the heaviest traffic flow. I quickly relieved Billy of his duties, but he never gave up the names of those friends who put him to work that evening.

Either of these situations could have turned deadly, but fortunately, for everyone's sake, they did not. Just as fortunate, the incidents involving Billy and friends gradually stopped occurring, or at least I never became aware of any other incidents.

CHAPTER 19

THEFTS

T hefts on campus are probably the most frequently reported crime and, unfortunately, many go unsolved each year. It requires an extremely proactive campus police department to prevent thefts, reduce the number of thefts that occur, and/or solve those that *are* reported. The following are a few examples of specific thefts I encountered over the years.

Not Ernie's Umbrella

It was a cold, rainy fall morning, when a female student walked into my office and reported that someone had stolen her umbrella. Naturally, because it had been raining, she carried the umbrella into the classroom and left it to dry in a back corner of the room. The theft took place approximately ten minutes before she reported the crime. At first, I figured this would be a tough crime to solve because everyone on campus was carrying an umbrella; after all, it was raining. However, the longer the victim described the event, the more I realized we had a chance. The student's father sold and installed elevators in buildings throughout the state. With every elevator he installed, he gave the owner a complimentary umbrella. The umbrella was blue with the company logo plastered visibly on the exterior.

Since the cafeteria was scheduled to open for lunch at any time, I assigned an officer to stand at the front door and watch for anyone carrying the umbrella. Sure enough, right on schedule, in walked Ernie with the umbrella. The officer escorted Ernie to my office, where I promptly read him his rights. Unbelievably, he waived his right to counsel and agreed to speak with me. I began the conversation in an unusual way; simply, I asked him if he or anyone in his family owned a multi-story building in the state.

Perplexed, he replied, "No."

I gave him a second chance, "Are you sure Ernie?"

"No, no one in my family owns anything like that."

I continued, "Have you, in the recent past, purchased an elevator, or know anyone who has?"

Now he was aggravated, "No."

I told Ernie the story the victim had just reported, and asked him if he could help me decide the direction I should take. I asked if he thought I should charge the person who committed the theft on a campus judiciary level, or if he thought I should make a criminal arrest. The aggravation melted into remorse (at least for being caught).

Ernie lowered his head, "Please don't arrest me, sir."

You would think Ernie's life of crime would have ended there, but circumstances made it such that he would continue. When found guilty of the theft mentioned earlier, he received a sentence of disciplinary probation, and a small fine of fifty dollars. The theft of an umbrella might seem insignificant, until you factor in circumstances Ernie was dealing with that we were not aware of at the time.

I found later as I was charging Ernie with a second theft, stealing from his roommate, that he had also been suspended from the football team for failing grades, had fallen several payments behind on his phone bill, and his girlfriend was pregnant. These combined factors led him to steal from his roommate, a person with whom he had previously had a good relationship.

Ernie was again found guilty, suspended, and to my knowledge, never returned to college. The point is that one never knows what mitigating factors are occurring in someone else's life. Someone you expect to trust could just as easily become someone who will stop at nothing to better his or her own financial position. Was Ernie a bad person? No, Ernie was a young man who felt he had no other option but to resort to criminal activity to make ends meet.

TEXT BOOK THEFTS

If you have not learned this by now, you will shortly after your son or daughter arrives on campus—textbooks are extremely expensive. Textbooks are also extremely easy to steal. Students are often encouraged by bookstore personnel to refrain from writing their names in books because it reduces their value during book buy-back days at the end of the semester. Many students listen to this misguided advice. Instruct your student to write their initials in small print at the top of a certain page in each textbook. If they do this, and the book is later stolen, it will be easier for campus police to identify the property.

Textbooks are prime targets of thieves during the first weeks of a semester. Unfortunately, many students arrive on campus only to learn that books are crazy expensive, and there is no hope of finding the necessary funds with which to purchase books before classes are underway. Those students who are able to purchase books as classes begin should make note of those students in class who do not have a book within the first week or so. If a theft occurs, one of these students might suddenly have a textbook. It happens. If the book was not stolen from *your* student, it more than likely once belonged to someone else in your student's class.

As the semester winds down, and book salespersons arrive on campus to buy back used textbooks, thieves seem to flourish even more. Maybe for good reason too, as everyone is usually running short on funds, and trying to find ways to travel home for the Christmas holidays, or summer break. Be especially cautious of the weeks prior to finals each semester. You may have found yourself in the habit of leaving books lying about unattended at the cafeteria, or even in your room with the door unlocked when you were out visiting someone else on your hall; and you were able to do so without losing anything earlier in the school year. Know that things change a great deal towards the end of the semester. A person living across the hall from you during the entire school year now becomes the person who finds himself or herself in possession of your books, about to cash them in for traveling money at the campus bookstore.

DORM THEFTS

One of the most frequently occurring crimes on campus is that of dorm theft. You can count on it happening from the opening days of the semester, and through the remainder of the school year.

During summer orientation sessions, I always mention to incoming freshmen and parents that thefts will occur unless students protect themselves. This includes engraving valuables, maintaining a list of property such as computers, stereos, radios, and so forth by make, model, general description, and serial numbers. Reporting a theft without providing the campus with this information drastically reduces the chances of recovery. If an ounce of prevention is worth a pound of cure, so goes it with preventing dorm theft.

When freshmen arrive on campus, they bring with them a carload of the valuables mentioned above. Having the desire to fit in with everyone in the dorm, it is common for fellow students to be invited in to enjoy games, music, and so forth. Having the latest and hottest video games is an especially cool way to make new friends. What most students fail to realize though, even after being warned, the students and other people they encounter in the first few weeks of school are not friends, but acquaintances. It takes a long time for a relationship to develop into a friendship wherein a student can trust the other person with their property. Acquaintances will steal from you, simple as that.

Non-students also use the first few weeks of school to float through the halls, checking out the new arrivals and what they brought with them to campus. These people are often mistaken for fellow students, until it is too late. Some that I will mention shortly are gifted at meeting and greeting new students, only to target certain ones from the start.

By the time the semester is only four to six weeks underway, the campus police can readily identify students, and the vehicles they drive. At the same time, campus police have a good idea who is a student and who is not. It is the first few weeks of a semester, when everyone looks much the same, that non-students find it easy to operate on campus, stealing from trusting freshmen. If parents and campus police could convince students of one critical component in keeping themselves and their property safe, especially during the first weeks of school, it would be to call campus police to report strangers or suspicious behavior. Allow the police to check these people out to be certain they belong on campus.

Even if a student invites someone to campus, it does not necessarily mean the person is not going to create a problem of some sort of another. I believe people who have been invited to campus commit many thefts, and the inviting student may not even know their visitor is up to mischief. It has happened too many times over the years to discount it as something that will not happen again. If you see someone hanging around the residence hall, and they do not appear to be with anyone, call campus police and let them look into it further. If the person is a legitimate guest, and not involved in some sort of criminal activity, the campus police will be able to alleviate your concerns.

Carl's Visits to Campus

Carl enjoyed meeting new students on campus. He often hung out behind the student center after the evening meal hours, talking to students as they left for their dorms. Students naturally liked Carl; he was friendly and welcoming.

He was also a criminal.

Carl's story was that he lived off campus, attending classes as a commuter student. He targeted freshmen males. Carl was consistent in all manner of things, including the numerous breaking and entering violations he committed. I arrested him for twenty-three break-ins on campus.

After meeting students and learning where they lived, Carl would visit their rooms to play video games or hang out. He was fun to hang around and showed interest in their activities, especially their class schedule and traveling plans. Carl claimed he wanted to know so that he could see them off, or even meet them upon their return to campus after the weekend. What he really wanted to know was when their dorm would be empty so he could rob them blind.

How was Carl able to carry out so many break-ins? Simple. Whenever Carl became acquainted with a student and visited their room, he would always find a way to unlock the window while he was visiting. After the student left for the weekend, Carl would crawl through the unlocked window and steal their valuables. At each crime scene, our officers would discover that the victim was missing a pillowcase, an array of valuables and clothes, and the window would be ajar about one inch.

Carl was eventually sentenced in a criminal court to ten years in prison. About two years after Carl went to prison, we began having reports of break-ins, and the method of operation (MO) fit Carl's. I even made a comment when investigating one of these crimes that, "If Carl were not in prison, I would bet my last dollar that he was the one who committed this crime."

I called the prison department the following day and learned that Carl had been released two weeks earlier due to over-crowding in the prison. It took me about two to three more break-ins, and about as many weeks to find and arrest Carl once again.

The last time I checked he was still in prison. I hope that when he is released the next time, he will have grown too old to blend in with the student population or crawl through windows!

As difficult as the first few weeks of classes are for freshmen, even more so are the times immediately preceding break periods such as fall break, Thanksgiving and Christmas holidays, spring break, and the week of final exams. The likelihood of becoming a victim of dorm theft greatly increases during these times, where many students prepared to drop out of school due to failing grades, or other pressures. Oftentimes these students are preparing to return home, which could be hundreds of miles away and possibly in different states. Some of these students take the opportunity to steal from students who used to be considered friends. Many times these thefts are not discovered until the perpetrator has left the campus for places unknown.

Solving thefts at these times during a school year are difficult, at best. Many remain unsolved, even though the identity of the thief is known, because of geography. Trying to question someone who has left the campus and perhaps now residing in another state is near impossible. At times, I have made requests of law enforcement agencies in other locales to do a "knock and talk" at a suspect's residence. The response typically given is that they will see what they can do. I know most agencies are too busy to help, especially if the crime is not a serious felony.

CAMPUS DANCES

School dances often held on Thursday nights. At one school we discovered non-students coming to the dance, supposedly by invite, then creating problems shortly afterwards. As we began looking for ways to prevent this from reoccurring, we learned that students coming to the dances were often intimidated at the door by non-students looking for an invite. Most students would agree to invite the non-student inside, knowing that once inside they would distance themselves from the unwanted guests. After finding this to be a common occurrence, we began requiring students to provide a list of invited guests prior to the dance. Another method to eliminate this problem was that we began requiring guests to present a valid driver's license, which they had to surrender upon entering the dance. The license could not be retrieved until the guest left the dance for the night. These simple measures prevented many problems in our campus dances, and created a much safer atmosphere for our students and their legitimate guests.

BICYCLE THEFTS

It was common for bicycles to be stolen on campus. Far too often, students would leave their bicycle unattended and unchained. It was too tempting a target for local thieves who might be visiting the campus looking for such an opportunity. We very rarely were successful in recovering the stolen bikes, as the owners seldom had proof of ownership, such as bills of sale or serial numbers.

Many times, too, those who stole bicycles might steal three or four, strip the bikes down and make one very different looking bicycle from the harvested parts. Often, when we experienced a rash of bicycle thefts, we would later find bits and pieces of the stolen bikes in trash piles near the campus.

So naturally, when a student came into the office one evening and reported his bicycle stolen only moments before, I was quick informed him we would be extremely lucky to recover the bike, at least in one piece. Nonetheless, I started on patrol to see if I could spot the bike and the thief.

Typically, these searches were unproductive, so my expectations were low as I left the office. I knew it would have to be the absolute best-case scenario in order to recover the stolen bike, because more often than not, the bikes were cannibalized immediately after being stolen.

We were more fortunate this time.

Elwood's Joyride

Elwood was an all-American football player, whose six-foot seven-inch height and three-hundred plus pounds was intimidating to any who might stand next to him. Because of his build, he stood out as he rode a bicycle away from the cafeteria only moments before the theft was reported. I found out later, as Elwood readily admitted the theft to me, that he had suffered a long, difficult practice session on the football field and he was simply too tired to walk back to the dorm after dining in the cafeteria.

Elwood was charged with a campus code violation, primarily because he readily admitted the theft and because the bicycle was returned undamaged (other than the tires perhaps being a bit flatter). In addition, this was the first occasion in four years that this student had ever encountered campus police in a negative manner. Although he was huge compared to most people on campus, he was never one to throw his weight around in order to intimidate other students. Had I been able to charge him with being somewhat arrogant on this occasion, I would have, but instead he received a campus judiciary charge in which a hefty fine was levied.

I imagine he did not find the fine too severe, and he surely recovered the funds a few years later when he played for a Super Bowl Champion team.

SALT WATER THEFTS

We began experiencing a rash of breaking and entering crimes to soft drink vending machines one year. The puzzling part was that there was no evidence a crime had even been committed. It began when one vendor reported a machine was empty of drinks and money, but there was no sign of forced entry. When I went to the location and checked the machine, there was no sign of anything out of the ordinary, except that a small pool of water running out from under the machine. Another day passed and yet another vendor reported a similar theft. Then vendors began reporting, to the local police, that machines around town had also been emptied. With each one, there was one similarity, a pool of water standing at base of the machine.

I would like to say that it was good police work, and partly because of the **WANTED** fliers I posted around campus, that led to solving this crime, but mostly it was plain old human nature. Apparently, the thieves did not share with someone who happened to catch them in the act of emptying a machine.

A student was sitting in his room one evening, with the door ajar, when he noticed several students running down the hall carrying armfuls of soft drinks. He knew something was up, so he followed the students to their room. There he noticed that the room was filled with soft drinks. He asked for a few drinks for himself, but was abruptly told, "No!" A short while later, an anonymous caller told us to check a certain room and we would find evidence of the recent breaking and entering referred to on the fliers that were posted in the residence hall.

After questioning the suspects, I learned that a warm, salt-water mixture was poured into the coin slot of the machines, which created an electrical short and caused the machine to empty itself of drinks and coins. I am not sure the students realized the act also corroded the machine and destroyed the electrical components. Each student was charged on a campus judiciary level, arrested, required to reimburse the vending company in the neighborhood of ten thousand dollars, and then suspended from school. The lesson proved to be quite costly.

THEFT OF RENTAL PROPERTY

Shelby was a student employee who had worked in our department for several years. He had a great personality and was always quick with a smile. It was a pleasure having him working in the department. One afternoon, a female non-student walked into my office and said that she wanted to report a theft. When she named Shelby as the culprit, I was more than alarmed. As she told her story, I realized that she and Shelby had been romantically involved and that, after renting a television from a local rental company, she loaned it to Shelby for his dorm room. When the relationship ended, Shelby decided to keep the television. I informed the young woman that I would make an effort to recover her property immediately.

I sent word for Shelby to come to my office. When he arrived, Shelby was very defensive about the television, stating that the former girlfriend had given it to him, and that he was not going to return it. He did not know at the time it was a rental, only that it showed a good quality picture.

When I explained to him that it had to be returned or that someone had to pay for the property in order to keep it, he quickly told me that he would pay for it. I had already written out on a sheet of scrap paper how much the television would cost. When he realized that it would cost more than $200 to cover the past-due rental fees, and that for that same amount he could buy a brand new one, he turned the property over to his former friend.

CHAPTER 20

VANDALISM

I have mentioned several times, that I was never shocked at the different things college students did over the years. That does not mean I was not taken aback a time or two. Just when I thought I had seen everything, something would happen that reminded me I still had a lot to learn. The American college student is young, creative, and always willing to devise a plan to bring down the house.

DORM VANDALISM

Students have been rolling vehicles with toilet paper or marking the windshields with soap since the dawn of time. Just as often, a dorm room might have the door penny-jammed so the occupant could not open the door from the inside. When that gets boring, they spray talcum powder under the door, filling the room with white powder. These types of vandalism, if not done repeatedly to the same person as a malicious prank, are typically considered harmless fun. There are other occasions where the fun comes at a price, and a seemingly innocuous incident becomes a crime.

More than once a call came in to our office wherein a student had tried to unlock his/her dorm room and the key would not fit into the lock. Upon arrival, our officers usually discovered that glue had been forced into the locking mechanism, requiring maintenance to come, remove the lock, and replace it with a new one. This sort of crime was very seldom solved, and, thankfully, it was one that occurred even more seldom. There was a great deal of expense involved when maintenance had to be called back to work after hours, and when a lock was damaged to the point it was not repairable

TIRE VANDALISM

One school year, we experienced a rash of flat tires over the course of a two—to three-week period. A number of students reported having all four tires on their vehicles flattened. With each report, when officers arrived to investigate, they discovered that the tires had not been cut or slashed; someone had simply let the air out.

This was puzzling because the incidents were happening between the hours of 10pm-2am, a busy time on campus. With the vehicles typically parked on the main street, we could not understand how someone was taking the time to let out the air in all four tires, undiscovered. We reasoned it must have been at least four people involved in order to commit the crime and be gone so quickly. As luck would have it, and it was mostly that, we learned that one very-creative student was committing the crimes. One at a time, he would unscrew the valve stem cover on all four tires, place a small stone inside the cover and screw it back on the tire. This caused the air to leak from the tires over a two—to three-hour period. This bit of ingenuity provided ample time for the culprit to make a safe getaway, at least for a while.

FIRE VANDALISM

Fire is always a scary thought on a college/university campus, and though the buildings are most often brick and mortar, the contents within can burn and create deadly smoke. It was common to have trashcans set afire by someone tossing a burning cigarette into the receptacle and walking away. This was easily eliminated by prohibiting smoking in the residence halls, and something as simple as keeping trash containers emptied.

Whenever you visit a residence hall, and you notice an overfilled trash container(s), know that this should be brought to someone's attention in residence life immediately.

I don't know if this is a crime confined mostly to college /university campuses, but it was fairly often that we would have a student report his/

her vehicle as having been vandalized. Most times the vehicle in question would be <u>keyed</u> down one side or the other, and sometimes on both sides. Often, there would be the typical scratch running the full length of the vehicle. Other times there might be a name scratched into the paint. So many times the student would tell officers they did not have any idea who was involved.

Almost as often, we learned it was a former boyfriend or girlfriend, or someone else's boyfriend or girlfriend. I responded to scenes where vehicles had been painted, windshields busted, and hoods dented. You never knew what to expect until you responded to the scene and investigated.

One semester we had a situation that quickly infuriated the campus community, and it looked as if the campus police could not solve the crimes. In a period of one week, we discovered dozens and dozens of radio antennae broken off parked vehicles. The vandal did not simply bend them or break them off and leave them lying about the parking lot; no, the antennae were all snapped off at the base and carried away. I wondered what someone was doing with the antennae. We had encountered a similar problem in the past where vandals were breaking off hood ornaments of Mercedes, but I couldn't fathom what someone would want with random car antennae.

I could tell from the beginning that the antenna situation was something different. No particular make or model vehicle was targeted; and, I had never heard of this particular craze happening elsewhere in the country. Had it not been for one of the vandals getting a little carried away one evening and, thankfully, a student taking time to report a suspicious activity, we might never have solved this crime.

As it turned out, two students were involved in the crimes. It was later revealed they were having a contest to determine who could be the first to steal thirty antennae. An argument ensued between the two one evening, and when one tried stealing a few antennae from the other to boost his trophy collection, he was discovered. His accomplice started whipping him with an antenna, and when another student in the dorm witnessed the incident, he called the campus police.

At about the same time the radio antennae were being stolen, someone was also apparently jumping on the hoods of parked vehicles and leaving large dents. A number of vehicles showed similar damage, and the crimes appeared to have been randomly committed. None of the victims could be connected, and the incidents were occurring throughout the campus. I was not surprised when one of the antenna vandals gave a statement that implicated an associate with this most recent crime spree. I did not mention earlier, both types of crimes were committed after nightly drinking binges. The three students were flunking out and needed something to pass the time.

It is so important to identify students who are not attending classes and persuade them to either resume their classes or go home. The university where I last worked did an outstanding job with this. Professors worked with student affairs to identify students who were not attending class, and the students were then interviewed immediately. Those students with extra time on their hands, knowing they would be leaving school permanently, were usually involved in some sort of difficulty on campus. It helped me coin the phrase: "Be good or be gone!"

CHAPTER 21

FALSE REPORTS

Sometimes, and thankfully this occurs infrequently, there are occasions when students file false reports. However, I made it a policy (and I expected the same from those working under my authority) to consider every report legitimate unless proven otherwise. Too many times, I heard police officers sound skeptical when someone reported a crime, as if they had the right to make judgments without knowing all the facts. Thankfully, this sense of power was not prevalent among officers who worked in the departments I managed. A police officer's first duty is to render aid to someone in trouble. Whenever a student walked in and asked to report a crime, he/she was afforded every respect.

Joe Don't Play

Joe walked into my office one afternoon and reported that Tim and Jared had just assaulted him outside the dormitory. It was readily apparent he was speaking the truth, because he had visible bruising on his face, arms, and chest. I could tell he had definitely been struck a number of times. The difficult thing for me to comprehend in this situation was the two suspects he identified were student workers in the campus police department. I knew the alleged assailants personally.

When I contacted Tim and Jared and asked them to come to the office, they were not sure what I wanted. After reading both students their rights, I was informed that they had in fact tag-teamed Joe as he walked out of the dormitory only a short while earlier. As the two talked more about the alleged crime, I soon realized that it was not a crime at all, but a very, very rough game in which the victim was a willing participatant.

A few weeks earlier, a professional wrestling event had been held on campus and, after watching the performance, sixteen students decided to form tag-teams of their own. There were eight two-man teams in the unofficial wrestling league the students organized. The rules were simple. Any team could wrestle another team or member of an opposing team, at will. Joe and his partner had tag-teamed Jared less than an hour earlier. In the spirit of the "agreement", Joe was tag-teamed by Tim and Jared afterwards as he left the dorm.

When I spoke with Joe afterwards, he confirmed the stories that Tim and Jared had provided, saying that he was upset because he had been roughed up earlier. There were no resulting campus judiciary charges against any of these so-called wrestlers, but their unofficial league ended from that moment on.

The Girl Who Cried Wolf

Elizabeth came into my office one morning, sobbing and very much disturbed. She reported that the previous night, while visiting a friend in one of the male dorms, she was grabbed and dragged into a room, as she walked down the hallway. Once inside the room, she was forced onto a bed, and raped. The room was dark, and she was not able to provide any information other than the fact she was attacked by two males. Elizabeth was able to tell me the room in which the attack occurred, and that the attackers were African-American.

Elizabeth happened to be Caucasian.

I could care less about her race, but I knew in a small southern community, word of a white female being raped by two African-Americans would spread like wildfire. After determining that two African-American students (Ron and Don) did, in fact, live in the room Elizabeth pointed out, I asked the occupants to come to my office.

Once there, in separate interviews, both were read their rights, and both gave separate, but confirming statements. Both of these young men adamantly denied the rape accusation, but both reported that Elizabeth had entered their room upon invite the night before. According to their statements, the night before, during the dorm's normal visitation hours, Ron was standing in the open doorway of the room as Elizabeth walked past. Ron spoke to her and invited her into the room, and she accepted the invitation.

Both boys stated that Elizabeth was inside the room for less than a minute or two before stating that she had to leave.

I spent approximately forty hours interviewing the victim, the two suspects, and various students in the dorm, friends, and even several of Elizabeth's professors. I learned enough from the interviews that when I spoke with Elizabeth a final time, she admitted to making a false report. She was failing miserably in most of her classes, and she wanted to find a way to leave school without her parents knowing that she was failing. She dropped out of school the following day.

As I made mention earlier, I always considered every report legitimate unless proven otherwise by a thorough investigation. Those times when the report proved to be false, I never looked poorly upon the student who made the report. I understood that life for college freshmen is difficult at best, and that every student responds differently to the many different situations they face.

PART THREE

CRIME PREVENTION

CHAPTER 22

CRIME PREVENTION

E very campus police department should have a basic crime prevention program that offers various services for the campus population. The primary focus should be the safety of the campus community. Campus police cannot protect a campus on their own; preparedness is a combined effort between faculty, staff, and students to develop a safe campus environment.

Every campus should have a crime prevention officer (CPO), whose primary responsibility is the development and implementation of crime prevention programs. Having an officer whose primary purpose is to focus on crime prevention demonstrates the college or university's dedication to maintaining a safe, secure campus. The CPO officer should be an individual who is familiar and involved with students living on campus. A good CPO officer will visit the residence halls on a frequent basis and have regularly scheduled events in each hall throughout the school year. At the very least, a general safety presentation should occur in each of the residence halls within the first two weeks of the semester to cover incidents from prior years, and any incidents that may have recently occurred.

Keep in mind that many thefts take place within this two-week period. Students should be familiar with how to report crimes, suspicious persons, or other questionable behavior to campus police. This is also a great opportunity for the CPO to discuss the dangers of other crimes, such as hazing. A number of students are lost each semester due to this crime; most could be prevented if the CPO were to spend a few minutes talking with students in the first two weeks of school.

RECOMMENDED CRIME PREVENTION PROGRAMS:

Rape Prevention
Theft Prevention
Engraving Valuable Property
Drugs and Alcohol Awareness
Severe Weather Warnings and Alerts
Fire Safety
Emergency Evacuations
Reporting Criminal Activity
Code Blue Telephones
CCTV's
Timely Crime Bulletins/Warnings

When you are determining which college or university to attend, check into the programs offered. Make sure they are not just programs on a piece of paper; verify that each is a viable component of the campus community, as evidenced by administration's support. Without the administration's support, most of the best-designed programs fail to accomplish what they were designed to do because funding is not made available.

I dislike trying to compare the two schools wherein I worked; however, at the private school I had moral support for some of the programs I designed to help protect the campus, but not always the financial support. The story I often heard was there was only so much money to go around. I had a difficult time convincing the administrators at this school of the need to put their money where their mouth was.

With the state-funded university, I had a great deal of financial support for some of the programs, but not always the moral support by key administrators. Campus police can have the best-developed plans or programs in the world, and possess a great deal of financial resources; however, if key administrators fail to buy into the programs and offer their moral support, the ideas will fail. I do not know which is the lesser of two evils in this situation. Research the campus in order to find out what the true atmosphere is like. Try to determine what type of relationship exists between the campus police and key administrators in student affairs or business affairs. Learn more about the relationship the campus police has with the president or chancellor. If there are not sound relationships wherein each faction is working closely together, you are not going to see the safest possible campus.

CONCLUSION

T here you have it. After surviving almost thirty years in campus law enforcement, I have now only barely scratched the surface describing what you may experience on a college or university campus. I mentioned earlier that I was rarely shocked by what I encountered over the years. However, I must also mention the bad things I have described in the preceding pages involved an extremely small percentage of students.

I could, and perhaps should, make mention of the many wonderful things I observed, but that in itself would be another book entirely. I hope the information offered in this book will forewarn you, both parents and students, of just a few of the dangers that lurk around college/university campuses nationwide. I hope what you have read will help you and your student become part of the vast majority of students who find their college experience filled with grand moments and fond memories; enough to last a lifetime and then some.

During my career, I felt good about the service I provided as a campus law enforcement leader. Writing this book allows me the opportunity to help those parents and students I might never meet.

Stay safe, and enjoy the college experience.

David L. Helton
Director of Police and Public Safety (Retired)

www.ingramcontent.com/pod-product-compliance
Lightning Source LLC
Chambersburg PA
CBHW050410290526
45786CB00003B/1197